# Gravity

Lisa Hill

Raintree

Chicago, Illinois

Customer Service  888-454-2279
Visit our website at www.heinemannraintree.com

Editorial: Megan Cotugno and Andrew Farrow
Design: Philippa Jenkins
Illustrations: KJA-artists.com
Picture Research: Ruth Blair
Production: Alison Parsons

Originated by Modern Age
Printed and bound in China by Leo Paper Group

13 12 11 10 09
10 9 8 7 6 5 4 3 2 1

**Library of Congress Cataloging-in-Publication Data**
Hill, Lisa.
Gravity / Lisa Hill.
    p. cm. -- (Sci-hi. Physical science)
  Includes bibliographical references and index.
  ISBN 978-1-4109-3250-1 (hc) -- ISBN 978-1-4109-3265-5 (pb)
  1. Gravity--Juvenile literature.  I. Title.
  QC178.H55 2008
  531'.14--dc22
                        2008026336

**Acknowledgments**
The author and publishers are grateful to the following for permission to reproduce copyright material: © Alamy/Mary Evans Picture Library p. **11**; © Alamy/Nick Turner p. **26**; © Alamy/Travis Rowan p. **iii** (Contents), p. **27**; © Charles Dermer p. **37**; © Corbis/Bettmann p. **25**; © NASA pp. **8, 20, 29, 30, 32**; © NASA Goddard Space Flight Center p. **34**; © iStockphoto pp. **4, 13, 15, 16, 18**; © PhotoDisc/StockTrek pp. **iii** (Contents), **6, 23, 28**; © Science Photo Library/Allan Morto/Dennis Milon p. **35**; © Science Photo Library/Roger Harris p. **39**; © Shutterstock pp. **11**, background images and design features throughout

Cover photographs reproduced with permission of © Corbis/moodboard **main**; © Science Photo Library/Julian Baum **inset**.

The publishers would like to thank literacy consultants Nancy Harris, Patti Suerth, and Monica Szalaj, and content consultant John Pucek for their assistance in the preparation of this book.

Every effort has been made to contact copyright holders of any material reproduced in this book. Any omissions will be rectified in subsequent printings if notice is given to the publisher.

Some words are shown in bold, **like this**. These words are explained in the glossary. You will find important information and definitions underlined and in bold, **like this**.

# Contents

How did gravity help create this huge crater? Find out on page 23!

How would the spring tide affect this surfer? Go to page 27 to find out!

# What Is Gravity?

SPLAT! Liquid from a bottle falls to the ground. Why didn't it fall up? Gravity pulled the liquid down to Earth. You cannot see or touch gravity. <u>Gravity is a pulling force all around us.</u>

## Universal Glue

Gravity is the glue that holds the universe together. Scientists call gravity the **force of attraction**. All objects, big or small, pull on each other. For example, Earth's gravity pulls on things close to its surface. Jump up from the ground, and Earth's gravity pulls you down.

Gravity is the force pulling this liquid down.

# Mass

**Gravity depends on two things— mass and distance.** Mass is how much matter or "stuff" there is in something. Dust particles, planets, and people have mass. One object is attracted to another object because of its mass. Gravity is the pulling force between two objects because of mass.

# Distance

Distance is a measurement of how far objects are from each other. If two objects are close to one another, their gravity will pull on each other. When they are far apart, they will feel less pull between them. We feel Earth's gravity because we live on Earth. If we lived in space, we would be distant from Earth. As you travel away from Earth into space, the pull of Earth's gravity becomes weaker.

Gravity keeps the Moon in orbit around the Earth. It also keeps the Earth in orbit around the Sun.

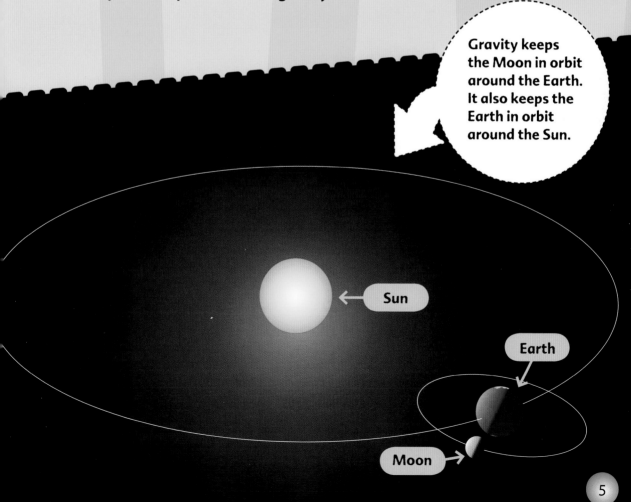

Sun

Earth

Moon

# Measuring Gravity

Earth has **mass**. Earth pulls all objects towards its center. But objects also pull on Earth. Smaller objects are pulled towards objects with more mass. Larger objects also feel the same pull from smaller objects. Every object has mass and a **force of gravity**. Since your body has mass, your force of gravity pulls on Earth.

Earth has mass and pulls all objects towards its center.

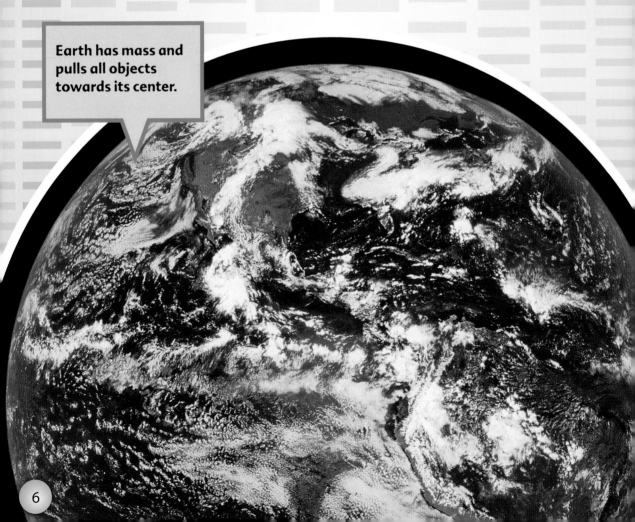

# Measuring Weight

Earth's force of gravity pulls on your body. We measure this effect of gravity as **weight**. Weight is the measurement of the force of gravity between two objects. A weight scale measures the pulling force, or the force of attraction (gravity), between two objects. Your weight measures the force of gravity between you and Earth.

# Mass and Gravity

The mass of an object is the same wherever it is. But, if one object has more mass than another, it will feel more gravity. Double the mass of one object, and the pull of gravity doubles.

<u>To increase gravity, you need to increase mass.</u> An elephant feels more gravity than a human, since it has more mass. The elephant's mass pulls more on Earth, and Earth's force of gravity pulls more on the elephant. Therefore, an elephant has more weight. If the distance between Earth and the elephant does not change, the weight of the elephant will increase if its mass increases.

## TRY THIS: WHAT DO OBJECTS WEIGH?

You can measure weight of objects with a bathroom scale.

Supply List: bathroom scale, paper, pencil, books.

1. Draw a table on paper to record your predicted and actual weight for individuals and books.

2. Predict your weight. Stand on the scale and weigh yourself. Stand on one foot on the scale. Do you weigh more or less? Or maybe the same?

3. What is the weight of a book? Weigh it.

4. Now, can you predict the weight of 2, 3, or 4 books? Weigh them and see if you were correct.

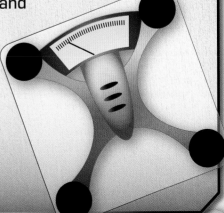

# Distance and Gravity

As objects travel thousands of kilometers from Earth, the force of gravity weakens. Earth's surface is about 6,378 kilometers (3,963 miles) from its center. Take, for example, a ball that weighs one kilogram (2.2 pounds) on Earth. Travel an additional 6,400 kilometers in space, and the ball is two times the distance from Earth's **core** (about 12,750 kilometers, or 8,000 miles). The ball will only weigh ¼ of its weight (0.25 kilogram, or 0.55 pound).

# Planets and Distance

Mass and gravity also affect the **revolution** of the eight known planets in our solar system that **orbit** the Sun. **A planet's revolution period is the time it takes to travel once around the Sun.** Because the Earth has a revolution period of 365.26 days, our calendar has an extra day (February 29) every four years to adjust. We call this a leap year. Why do the other planets take longer, or shorter, to make their revolutions? The answer involves distance!

On the Moon, this astronaut feels little gravity.

# Revolution!

Look at the table below. Mercury, the closest planet to the Sun, has the shortest revolution period. Neptune, the farthest planet from the Sun, has the longest revolution period. It is close to 165 years! Now, remember the rule of distance when it comes to gravity. When you increase the distance between the two objects, the force of gravity weakens.

Double the distance between two objects (in this case the Sun and a planet), and the force of gravity is ¼ of what it was. Triple the distance, and gravity is $\frac{1}{9}$ of what it was, and so on. So, a planet that is farther from the Sun will have a longer revolution period. A planet that is closer to the Sun will have a shorter revolution period.

| Planet | Revolution Period |
|--------|-------------------|
| Mercury | 87.97 days |
| Venus | 224.7 days |
| Earth | 365.26 days |
| Mars | 1.88 years |
| Jupiter | 11.86 years |
| Saturn | 29.46 years |
| Uranus | 84.01 years |
| Neptune | 164.79 years |

# Isaac Newton

**Over 340 years ago, Sir Isaac Newton explained how the force of gravity worked on Earth and in our solar system. Today, we use Newton's theory on gravity and his explanation of working forces.**

## A Young Genius

Isaac Newton was born in 1642. His family lived on a small farm in England. When he was 17, an uncle convinced his mother that Isaac Newton would never be a farmer. Newton's mother let him attend Trinity College in Cambridge, England. However, he had to help pay his school tuition by waiting on tables and cleaning rooms. During the summer of 1665, Trinity College closed down for two years. Newton returned home. Instead of idling his days away from college, Newton taught himself astronomy, math, and physics.

One summer day in 1665, young Isaac Newton sat in his garden drinking tea. History tells us Newton watched an apple fall to the ground. Newton thought that a certain force pulled on the apple. This same force could also pull on the moon and planets **orbiting** in space. **Isaac Newton did not discover gravity, but he explained how gravity worked.**

Newton's work also led to many other important discoveries. For example, using a simple glass prism, he demonstrated that white light could be split into many different colors. Newton had discovered the **color spectrum**.

Newton explained that the same force pulling on this apple was responsible for the orbiting planets.

What did Newton discover about gravity? Find out on the next page!

# Newton's Laws of Motion

To understand gravity, Isaac Newton studied how objects moved on Earth and in space. He created the laws of movement and simple forces to help us understand gravity better.

# Newton's First Law of Motion: The Law of Inertia

**An object that is not moving will stay still until acted upon by a force.** A still object will resist change (it will not move). This property, or action, is called **inertia**. How does inertia work? Objects that do not move remain still. Take for example a soccer ball sitting on a field. It requires the force of a player to move it.

If pushed or pulled, objects will move and keep moving at the same speed and same direction. A second action or force is required to make this object change direction and speed. This is Newton's **Law of Inertia**.

A ball on the field does not move. Kick the ball and it moves in one direction and speed.

# Newton's Second Law of Motion: The Law of Resultant Force

Newton also studied how objects **accelerate**, or change their speed. <u>If an object is pushed or pulled with a force, its speed or direction will change.</u> Acceleration depends on an object's mass and the force acting on it. A force can change the direction or speed of that object. This is Newton's **Law of Resultant Force**.

A rocket sits on a launch pad. Earth's gravity pulls the rocket to the ground. The rocket engines ignite. Gradually, the rocket rises into the sky. The force of the engines is stronger than Earth's force of gravity. The rocket starts to accelerate. As the rocket travels away from Earth, it feels less gravity. The rocket also burns up heavy fuel. It has less mass. With less mass and less pulling gravity, the rocket's acceleration increases and it flies faster.

# Gravity and Acceleration

**We can measure the effect of gravity as weight, but how is gravity measured as a force?**

Scientists measure this force as a **Newton**. A Newton is the force required to move one kilogram (kg) of mass as it accelerates one meter (m) per second per second ($s^2$).
The formula is written (x = multiplication):

**1 Newton = 1 kg  x  m/s$^2$**

**Gravity pulls objects down to Earth with a constant acceleration.**
This means a falling object will travel faster and faster at a constant acceleration, or 9.8 m/s$^2$. It will accelerate, or increase speed, no faster or slower unless acted upon by a different force (as explained by Newton's Laws of Motion). Acceleration due to Earth's gravity is the constant (g).
The formula is written:

**g = 9.8 m/s$^2$**

To measure this force in Newtons, we use this formula:

**Force = mass x acceleration**

If you dropped a 10 kg ball from a tower, the ball would accelerate, or increase speed, from Earth's gravity at 9.8 m/s$^2$.
What is the force working on this ball?

**Force = 10 kg   x  9.8 m/s$^2$ = 98 Newtons**

The ball is experiencing 98 Newtons of gravitational force while falling to the ground.

You can test this by dropping objects from different heights. Does gravity make heavy objects move faster?

Supply List: similar shape and size objects, such as a glass marble and a small pom-pom ball (each 14 mm or ½ inch), a ping-pong ball and golf ball, a tennis ball and orange, one stopwatch, one pencil, one piece of paper

1. Draw a chart on paper, so you can write down your test results.

2. Drop the lighter objects first (marble and pom-pom ball).

3. Drop at different heights.

4. Have a partner hold the stopwatch. Time each pair of objects dropped.

5. Write down the drop time for each pair of objects.

Objects of similar shape and mass should drop at the same speed. Gravity pulls on the mass of each object.

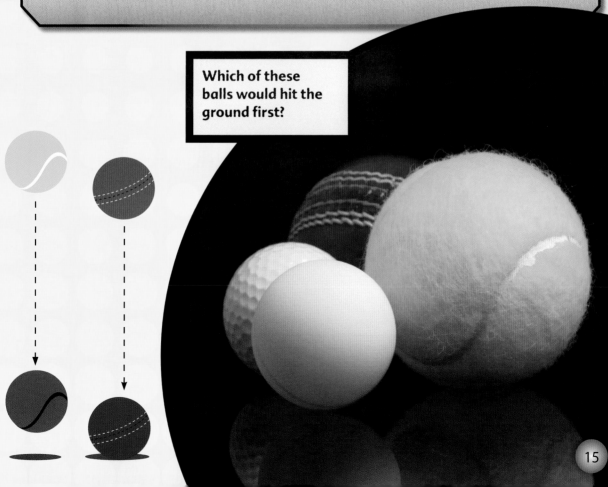

Which of these balls would hit the ground first?

# Gravity At Work

A snowboarder streaks across the snow. He rockets through a half pipe and shoots into the air. He hangs effortlessly in the sky, yet **gravity** pulls him towards Earth. What goes up must come down!

Gravity is one of the forces pulling on this snowboarder.

# Streaking Meteors

Earth's gravity pulls in space **particles** and other objects through its **atmosphere**. A comet streaks across space. Bits of comet dust and ice are left in its blazing, white-blue trail. As Earth orbits through the comet's path, comet particles are drawn in by Earth's gravity. Comet particles flash across Earth's atmosphere as burning meteors (shooting stars). The meteors burn up, traveling faster than any supersonic jet.

# Pulling Particles

Can gravity work on tiny particles? All objects in the universe contain matter. Matter is made of tiny particles. Gravity is always on and never stops working. **Gravity attracts small particles of matter together to make bigger objects.** This is why gravity is called the **force of attraction**.

**Wow!**

- ▶ Gravity can make hard boiled eggs stand up on end. Use sandpaper to smooth the egg's bottom. Carefully stand the egg up on a table. Be patient!

- ▶ In space, astronauts can grow about two inches taller. There is little or no gravity to compress, or pull down on their bones. Back on Earth, they shrink to their normal height.

- ▶ If you get caught in an avalanche, sometimes it is hard to identify which way is up or down. Try spitting a little saliva out of your mouth. It will run downward. Gravity always pulls down!

# CAN tHe FoRCe OF GRaViTY Change?

To change **gravity** on Earth, the planet's **mass** would have to change. Earth's mass would have to increase or decrease. How would Earth's mass change? Meteorites landing on Earth add mass. However, it would take many meteorites to detect an increase in Earth's mass.

## Gravity Turned Off

What if gravity was turned off? You could jump off the Earth. You would have no weight. Throw a ball, and it could travel to the Moon.

This barbell would float away if gravity was turned off.

You can show that falling objects are pulled by gravity at the same acceleration, or increasing speed. Here is how!

Supply List: two pennies, one medium-sized rubber band, two assistants, flat table

1. On the table, one assistant holds a rubber band with two fingers (like a slingshot). Place the penny inside the rubber band. Pull one section of the rubber band back with the penny.

2. A second assistant holds a second penny out from the table (at equal height with the first penny).

3. Watch the two assistants. At the count of 3, ask your two assistants to release their pennies.

Both pennies will land at the same time. Gravity pulls with equal force on objects of the same mass!

# Double Gravity

What if the **force** of gravity doubled? Buildings might collapse from the extra force. Structures are constructed for normal gravity, not extra gravity. Trees would break. People would weigh twice as much. <u>**Weight is a measurement of gravity's pulling force between two objects.**</u>

Wow!

**During a full moon, the Sun and Moon's combined gravitational pull may draw more magma out of active volcanoes on Earth.**

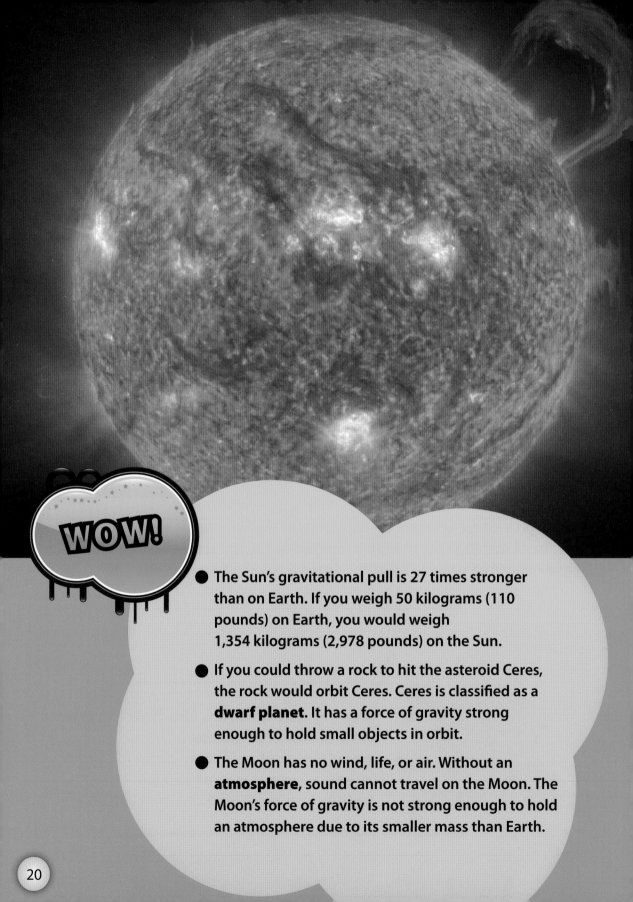

**WOW!**

● The Sun's gravitational pull is 27 times stronger than on Earth. If you weigh 50 kilograms (110 pounds) on Earth, you would weigh 1,354 kilograms (2,978 pounds) on the Sun.

● If you could throw a rock to hit the asteroid Ceres, the rock would orbit Ceres. Ceres is classified as a **dwarf planet**. It has a force of gravity strong enough to hold small objects in orbit.

● The Moon has no wind, life, or air. Without an **atmosphere**, sound cannot travel on the Moon. The Moon's force of gravity is not strong enough to hold an atmosphere due to its smaller mass than Earth.

# Gravity Quiz

1. What is gravity?

2. Why do we feel gravity?

3. Is there gravity in space?

4. How does gravity work?

5. What is mass?

6. What is the Law of Inertia?

7. Is gravity always working?

8. Can gravity change?

9. Does a heavy rock feel more gravity than a light rock?

10. Can you see gravity?

See page 43 for quiz answers.

# The Solar System

For billions of years, clouds of dust and gas swirled in space. Slowly, gravity pulled the dust and gas particles together to form stars. <u>Gravity also pulled together particles of dust, gas, and rocks to make planets.</u>

## Our Star

The Sun is a massive burning ball of gas and the center of our solar system. More than one million Earths could fit inside the Sun. The Sun's gravitational field extends trillions of kilometers into space. Far distant planets, moons, **asteroids**, and comets **orbit** the Sun or are slowly being pulled in by the Sun's gravity.

## The Moon

In space, there are billions of solar systems and galaxies. Sometimes, a planet's gravity pulls in asteroids and comets. Some astronomers believe an object the size of Mars crashed into Earth billions of years ago. Pieces of Earth flew off into space. Gravity pulled this ejected material together to form Earth's natural satellite, the Moon. Other astronomers believe the Moon is a captured asteroid pulled in by Earth's gravity.

# TRY THIS: MEASURE A METEORITE IMPACT

Earth's gravity pulls in asteroids, comets, and meteors. If they hit Earth, they can form impact craters. A meteorite is the remains of a meteor that survived falling to Earth.

What do meteorite impacts look like? Does the size and mass of the meteorites make a difference? This is how you can find out:

Supply List: large plastic sheet, 10–12 cm deep box lid (photocopy paper box lid), white flour, cocoa powder, large plastic sheet, ruler, paper, pencil, similar sized objects with different mass (ping pong ball and golf ball, tennis ball and orange, 14 mm glass marble and pom-pom ball)

1. Spread a large plastic sheet on the floor. Put the box lid in the middle. Be careful, this activity can be messy.

2. Place approximately 6 cm of white flour on the lid bottom (about 4–6 cups of flour). Sprinkle a thin layer of cocoa powder on top to cover the white flour.

3. Drop projectiles of different mass and size from the same height level. Vary the heights.

4. Measure each crater's depth and width. Which made the deepest crater? Which made the largest crater?

A meteorite pulled on by Earth's gravity caused this impact crater.

# Galileo

**Galileo Galilei was an Italian scientist who lived from 1564 to 1642. He studied the heavens and gravity to explain how our solar system was created.**

As a young university student, Galileo didn't always believe what his teachers told him. Many professors taught that heavy objects fell faster than lighter objects. Galileo decided to prove them wrong. History tells us he climbed a tall, leaning tower in Pisa. He dropped a 0.45 kilogram (1 pound) lead ball and a 45 kilogram (100 pound) lead ball. Both objects landed at the same time. Galileo showed that objects fell at the same speed due to **gravity**.

# The Telescope Man

In 1610 astronomers informed people that Earth was the center of the universe. The Sun, Moon, and other planets revolved around Earth. Many years earlier, the astronomer Copernicus had tried to argue that Earth and the surrounding planets revolved around the sun. But his idea was criticized. Galileo was convinced that Copernicus was right.

Galileo had heard about an instrument that allowed distant objects to be seen up close. He was curious about this interesting toy, and decided to make one. He ground and set glass lenses inside an old organ pipe tube. With this new invention, the telescope, Galileo discovered four moons orbiting Jupiter. Through his observations, Galileo later proved that the Sun was the center of our solar system.

# Gravity's Pulling Force

You are on a river, and a huge wall of water rushes toward you. The wave travels so fast it looks like the water is moving backwards. This wave is called a tidal **bore**. In the United Kingdom, a tidal bore also surges up the Severn River. The rise and fall of Earth's oceans every day are called **tides**.

See the rush of the water coming towards you? It is a tidal bore, on the Severn River in the United Kingdom.

# Daily Tides

**Tides are formed from the pulling force of the Sun, Moon, and Earth's gravity.** Earth's gravity pulls the oceans close to its surface. The Sun and Moon also pull on the oceans. However, since the Moon is closer to Earth, the Moon's gravity affects the oceans more than the Sun. The Moon is also closer to the oceans than to the center of the Earth. Therefore, the Moon's force of gravity on the ocean is higher than the Moon's force of gravity on the Earth.

The moon's gravity pulls the oceans to form a tidal bulge. On the opposite side of the Earth is another tidal bulge. As Earth rotates, the bulging water follows the moon's gravity pull. Places on Earth pass through these tidal bulges and experience low and high tides.

# Spring Tides

Every month, there is a full moon and a new moon. **Spring tides** happen when the new moon and full moon line up with the Sun. The pull of the Sun and Moon's combined gravity is stronger. The increased force of gravity produces extremely high and low tides on the ocean. This makes for some great waves to surf!

Surfers take advantage of the tides to ride the waves of the ocean.

# Space Weight

Different planets have different amounts of mass. A large planet with more mass will have a stronger force of gravity. Smaller planets that have less mass will have less gravity.

What would you weigh on the Moon? Our Moon is a natural orbiting satellite. Earth's Moon is more than ¼ the size of Earth. Yet, it has only $\frac{1}{6}$ of Earth's mass. Since the moon has less mass, it has about $\frac{1}{6}$ the gravity of Earth. A 45 kilogram (100 pound) person on Earth would only weigh about 7.5 kilogram (16.7 pound) on the Moon.

A person weighing 45 kg (100 lb) on Earth would weigh 17 kg (37.5 lb) on Mars!

# Satellites

Without gravity, satellites could not **orbit** around Earth. Satellites travel in space at very fast speeds. Earth's gravity pulls on the satellites, causing them to orbit Earth. Satellites allow different forms of communication (Internet, television, and **Global Positioning System**) to reach across the world. The Hubble Telescope orbits Earth and transmits amazing images of galaxies and distant stars.

You will learn more about orbiting objects on the next page!

The space shuttle Endeavour releases two satellites. They will orbit the Earth because of gravity.

# Gravity and Orbiting Objects

The Moon **orbits the Earth. It has its own speed called orbital velocity. Orbital velocity is the speed and direction required for a satellite—or in this case the Moon—to maintain orbit around Earth and not be pulled in by Earth's gravity.**

**Inertia** of a moving body tends to make it move in a straight line, while the force of gravity pulls it down. The Earth's gravity is pulling on the Moon, but the Moon's orbital velocity is just fast enough to prevent Earth's gravity from pulling it in. <u>**The Moon's orbital path is a balance between its inertia and Earth's force of gravity.**</u>

Earth's gravity pulls on the Moon. But what prevents the Moon from being pulled in by this gravity?

# Orbital Velocity

A heavy rocket thunders overhead and speeds high into the sky. In space, rockets place communication satellites in orbit. Satellites look like they float as weightless toys. Yet they can travel at a speed of orbiting 27,359 kilometers/hour (17,000 miles/hour) 242 kilometers (150 miles) above Earth. Just like the Moon, Earth's gravity pulls satellites into orbit while they travel in space.

The Sun's mass tries to pull everything into its hot center. Luckily, the Sun is very far away. Its force of gravity is not strong enough to pull in surrounding planets and their moons. Planets have an orbital velocity (speed) that allows them to orbit the Sun and resist the Sun's gravity.

## TRY THIS: ORBITING THE MOON

This activity demonstrates the Moon's orbit around Earth and how Earth's gravity keeps the Moon close.

Supply List: 2–3 meter long string, tennis ball, tape

1. Throw the tennis ball straight out. Notice its direct flight.

2. Tie the string around the tennis ball. Tape it securely.

3. Hold the string and throw the ball out.

4. Circle the tennis ball around your head.

The string pulls on the ball with your pulling force. Your pulling force imitates gravity and keeps the ball circling around you.

# What is Microgravity?

A rollercoaster loops and dives. Your stomach feels like it is in your throat. If you floated off your seat, you felt **microgravity**, or very little gravity.

On Earth, we feel heavy because of gravity. Gravity gives us weight. In space and far from planets or moons, there is less gravity. Astronauts can float in the International Space Station (ISS) because they feel microgravity. In orbit, astronauts are in **free fall** and feel weightless. They experience **zero gravity**, or zero g. Astronauts in orbit have the same amount of mass as on Earth. Yet in free fall, they have zero weight (weightlessness), because they feel very little gravity.

# Microgravity at Work

The International Space Station travels very fast. It is orbiting Earth at about 25,200 kilometers/hour (15,500 miles/hour). Inside the space station, all objects travel at the same speed orbiting Earth. Everything experiences the same "falling state," or free fall towards Earth. This means they feel the same amount of gravity. On page 38, you can experience microgravity at work when you create your own free fall balloon.

In space, astronauts feel the effect of zero gravity.

## TRY THIS: WATER FREE FALL

You can see the effects of free fall by conducting the experiment:

Supply List: tall cup, water, bucket, scissors

1. Poke two small holes on either side of the cup (near the bottom). (Ask an adult to help you.)

2. Hold the cup over a bucket.

3. Pour water into the cup. Note how the water drains out of the cup.

4. Place two fingers to cover the side holes.

5. Fill the cup $\frac{2}{3}$ full. Make sure water does not leak out from the two side holes.

6. Hold the cup over the bucket. Drop the cup.

Did any water escape the full cup while falling? The water is falling at the same rate as the cup. The water is free falling with the cup. Since the water is weightless in relation to the cup, it does not flow out.

NASA operates a Zero Gravity Research Facility (Zero-G). Inside the building is a long, 142 meter steel vacuum chamber. Scientists drop objects inside the vacuum chamber to study free fall. It takes 5.18 seconds to fall 132 meters.

# Gravity Monsters

In space, there are strange places where nothing escapes, not even light. Their gravity is so strong they can pull in and devour stars, planets, and galaxies. Scientists call these gravity objects **black holes.** A black hole tears everything apart like a hungry tornado. When objects disappear into a black hole, they do not return to this universe.

What is a black hole? At one time, a black hole was a living star. Stars are glowing, hot **spheres** of mixed, burning gases. As stars age, they continue to burn up their fuel (gases). When all of their fuel burns up, what is left is the star **core**. If the star core is dense or heavy enough, its gravity causes the star core to sink inward. As a star core shrinks, its mass becomes even denser and very heavy. Gravity can make the star core sink into itself, pulling in the surrounding space and time. The dead star has now become a black hole in space.

If our sun collapsed, it would shrink to the size of a football field. Our sun would have a super heavy, dense core. As objects increase in mass, their force of gravity increases. This is why a black hole has a strong force of gravity.

A black hole's gravity even pulls in planets and galaxies!

# TRY THIS: CREATE YOUR OWN BLACK HOLE

Everything pulled into a black hole disappears from the universe. You can see how a black hole works.

Supply List: 11 cm wide terracotta planting pot, 23–27 cm long black balloon, small 5 mm beads, duct tape, scissors

1. Stretch the balloon 3–4 times. Cut 5 mm off the tip of the balloon.

2. Cut five 16–18 cm pieces of tape. Stretch the cut end of the balloon over the top of the pot. Tape the balloon edge firmly onto the pot.

3. Push the balloon end through the pot's bottom center hole. Tie a knot.

4. Tape the knot tightly to the pot bottom.

5. Roll one or two beads into your "black hole."

## Wow!

▶ Our solar system lies in the Milky Way Galaxy. Astronomers believe a super massive black hole lies at the center of the Milky Way Galaxy.

▶ Black holes have a special signature in space. Astronomers search for black holes where light and stars seems to disappear. And they search for places where **x-rays** and **gamma rays** (high energy radiation) are released.

The Milky Way Galaxy contains our planet. It might also contain a black hole.

# Scientists In Space

How do you locate something you cannot see?  You look for clues that you can observe and identify.

## Dr. Dermer: Astrophysicist

Dr. Charles Dermer is an **astrophysicist** for the U.S. Navy Research Lab. He works in the Space Science Division. Dr. Dermer hunts **black holes** by finding places where stars and light disappear, behind the blaze of **x-ray** and **gamma rays** when black holes are born. He searches for areas where **matter** and light fall into black holes.

Dr. Dermer is an expert on dying stars. He describes black holes as **gravity** engines. Scientists believe the energy released by gravity travels in waves. When stars no longer burn gas, what remains is a spent star core. When the spent core of a star collapses to make a black hole, the energy released from the gravity makes high-energy x-rays and gamma rays. The strong gravity field of the black hole bends space and time. It powers the black hole.

Why does Dr. Dermer study black holes? Black holes and pulsars (pulsing stars) give off high-energy particles and waves (x-ray and gamma rays). These high-energy waves of radiation can travel billions of miles through space. They can damage satellites and space ships. Scientists study high-energy gamma rays and x-ray waves to protect astronauts and spacecraft and to help understand our universe.

# Space Riddles

Here's a riddle about what Dr. Dermer studies. What is dark, but is not a black hole? Scientists have proof that something black exists between stars. It is dark, has matter, so they call it **dark matter**. Dark matter cannot be seen, but it has a strong force of gravity. Dark matter can be found inside galaxies and between stars.

Dr. Dermer grew up in the open plains of Midwestern United States. He loved to watch the stars and planets travel across the dark sky. To discover science, all you need is to be creative and have ideas. Science is about observing, or studying, what goes on around you.

As an astrophysicist, Dr. Dermer studies black holes and dark matter.

This is how you can experience microgravity with a bang!

Supply List: graph paper, large box, paper clips, 4–5 small rubber bands, small balloons, 227 gram (8 ounce) fishing weight, tape, scissors, strong needle, chair, cushion, an adult assistant

1. Blow up a balloon and tie it off. Tape the balloon to the interior of the box top.

2. Hook 4–5 thin rubber bands together to make two elastic strings.

3. Attach one end of each elastic string to the fish weight. Slide one paper clip on each free end of the two elastic strings.

4. Use the scissors to poke one hole through the box top on each side of the balloon.

5. Push one of the paper clips through each hole. Lay each paper clip flat and secure with tape. The fish weight on the two elastic strings will hang below the balloon.

6. Let the fish weight stretch the elastic string close to the box bottom.

7. On top of the fish weight, tape the needle's sharp end up to point at the balloon.

8. Climb onto the chair. You need to raise the box 2 - 3 meters above the ground. Make sure an adult is assisting you!

9. Drop the box onto the cushion.

How does gravity work with the rubber bands and weight? Gravity pulls on the fishweight, causing the rubber band to stretch. Drop the box. The fish weight travels at the same speed of the box. The fish weight experiences microgravity, or free fall. Because of this, the weight is not actually pulling on the rubber bands, and it floats in the box. The pin pops the balloon.

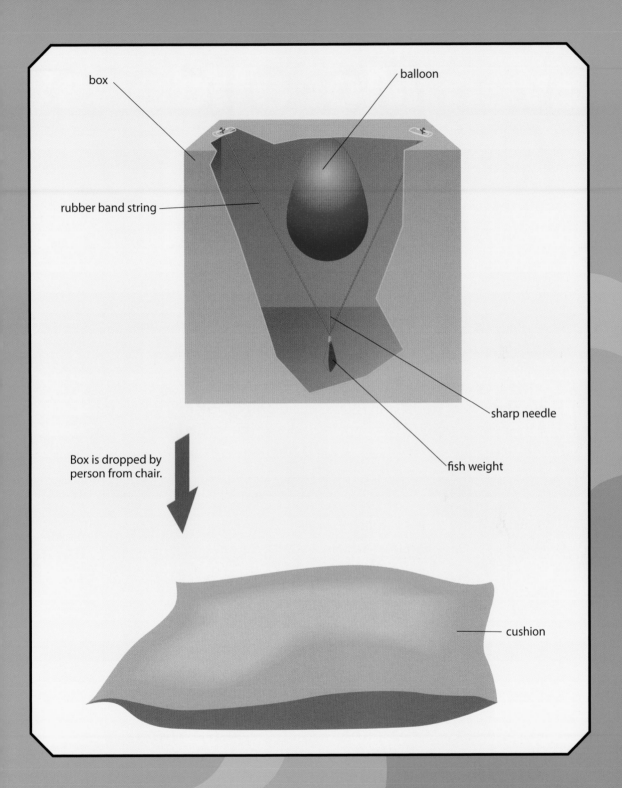

box

balloon

rubber band string

sharp needle

fish weight

Box is dropped by person from chair.

cushion

# Even More Ideas About Gravity

By studying the effects of **gravity**, scientists discover new ideas and inventions.

## Making the Heart Work

The heart pumps blood to different parts of your body. Gravity helps the heart work. Gravity pushes blood down, making the heart work to pump blood up. In space, there is less gravity. Astronauts have to exercise to keep the heart strong.

Scientists study how **microgravity** affects astronauts living out in space. Scientists look for signs that tell them when hearts may become lazy. Astronauts have to be healthy in order to explore space, or live on a space station.

## Bugs in Space

Glowing **bacteria** might someday tell you if you are sick. Scientists have found that bacteria and viruses grow better in microgravity. Some bacteria and viruses make us ill. Many of these bugs, however, keep us healthy. Special bacteria can be grown and tested in microgravity. If they detect a nasty chemical, gas, or bacteria, these unique good bacteria will glow. Tiny sensors will receive the bacteria's signal and warn scientists. Good bacteria will work in space to detect bad bacteria and toxic chemicals.

# "Warp Speed"

To travel in space requires extreme speed. Some jets can travel faster than the speed of sound at 1,230 kilometers/hour (760 miles/hour). To travel "warp speed" (like in the movies), spaceships would have to control gravity and travel faster than the speed of light 1.08 billion kilometers/hour (669 million miles/hour). We do not have this technology. **Astrophysicists** are still learning about gravity and light. There are many unanswered questions about how gravity works!

# Gravity Quiz 2

1. What is at the center of our solar system?

2. Why do planets orbit the Sun?

3. Why do satellites orbit Earth?

4. Do all planets have the same force of gravity? Why or why not?

5. What would you weigh on the Moon?

6. What is microgravity?

7. Can light escape a black hole?

8. Why do we study gravity?

9. Can we travel faster than the speed of light?

10. Do we fully understand gravity?

See page 43 for quiz answers.

# Quiz Answers

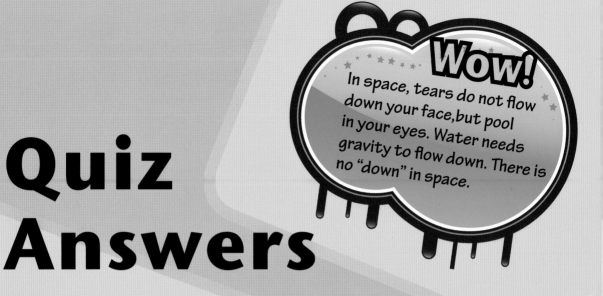

**Wow!**

In space, tears do not flow down your face, but pool in your eyes. Water needs gravity to flow down. There is no "down" in space.

## FROM PAGE 21

1. It is a pulling force between two objects.

2. Earth has more mass. We feel Earth's gravity pull.

3. Yes, gravity is also in space. But, distance weakens the force of gravity.

4. Gravity works based on two factors: mass and distance.

5. Mass is the amount of matter an object contains.

6. An object stays at rest or keeps moving unless acted upon by a different force.

7. Yes.

8. Yes.

9. Yes, the heavy rock has more mass and weight.

10. No, it is an invisible force.

## FROM PAGE 42

1. The Sun.

2. The Sun has a large mass, and its gravity pulls planets into orbit.

3. Their orbital velocity and Earth's gravity pulls them into orbit.

4. No, planets with more mass have a stronger force of gravity.

5. Multiply your weight by $\frac{1}{6}$. This is what you would weigh on the Moon.

6. It is the experience of a falling state, or free fall, towards Earth.

7. No, light cannot escape it.

8. We study it to learn how the universe was created.

9. No, we cannot.

10. No, gravity is a complicated force. Scientists continue to discover more about it.

# Gravity Timeline

**1609**    Galileo Galilei built the first astronomical telescope. By observing Jupiter and its gravitational pull on **orbiting** moons, Galileo proved that planets orbited the Sun.

**1686**    Sir Isaac Newton defined the Law of Gravity. Newton explained how gravity worked in relation to objects in space and on Earth.

**1705**    Sir Edmond Halley predicted the return of a comet (Halley's Comet). Halley used Newton's Law of Gravity to explain how the Sun's gravity captures comets. Comets have a predictable orbit around the Sun due to the Sun's **force** of gravity.

**1916**    Albert Einstein established his theory on how gravity shapes space and time flow. He called it General Relativity. By explaining how gravity can bend space and time, Einstein described how **black holes** are created from collapsing dead stars.

**1950**    Jan Oort discovered a giant cloud of comets surrounding the solar system. This huge **sphere** of frozen snowballs is called the **Oort Cloud**. Comets from the Oort Cloud are pulled in by the Sun's gravity to orbit our solar system.

**1969**    Neil Armstrong was the first man to walk on the Moon (*Apollo 11* mission). Due to the Moon's low gravity, astronauts weigh six times less than on Earth. Instead of walking, astronauts could leap across the Moon's surface.

**1990**    NASA launched the Hubble Telescope. Kept in orbit by Earth's gravity, the Hubble Telescope captures amazing photos of stars, galaxies, and the planets.

**2002**    A new **dwarf planet**, Quaor, was discovered 6.5 billion kilometers from the Sun. Quaor is located in the Kuiper Belt. This is a swarm of ice and rocky objects. Kuiper Belt objects are pulled in by the Sun's gravity to orbit the Sun.

**2004**    Astronomers discovered a second new dwarf planet, Sedna. Sedna is the coldest, most **distant** object known to orbit the Sun. Sedna lies in the Oort Cloud 12.9 billion kilometers from the Sun.

# Glossary

**Acceleration** A change in speed or direction

**Asteroid** Large piece of floating rock that formed at the same time as planets

**Astrophysicist** A space scientist who studies dark matter, dying stars, and black holes

**Atmosphere** The layers of gases that surround a planet

**Bacteria** Single-celled organism with no nucleus

**Black hole** A part of space where the gravitational field is so strong that nothing, not even light, can escape it

**Bore** A high wall of moving water caused by a very rapid rise of the tide in shallow, narrow channels

**Color spectrum** The series of colored bands arranged by their wavelengths; main colors are red, orange, yellow, green, blue, and violet

**Core** The central part of an object; like a star or planet

**Dark matter** A form of matter that is invisible; accounts for gravitational forces in the universe

**Distance** The amount of space between two things

**Dwarf planet** A planet which is too small to be considered a full planet

**Force** Push or pull that causes an object to start moving or changes the speed or direction of its motion

**Force of attraction** Another term for gravity

**Free fall** Fall of an object that is acted on only by gravity; an orbit is a form of free fall

**Gamma ray** A form of electromagnetic radiation

**Global Positioning System (GPS)** A system that uses satellites and radio waves to pinpoint locations on Earth

**Gravity** The force of attraction between all objects

**Inertia** The resistance of an object to being moved or to having its motion changed

**Law of Inertia** Newton's law that states that an object stays at rest or keeps moving in a straight line at a constant speed unless acted upon by a force

**Law of Resultant Force** Newton's law that states that an object tends to accelerate, or speed up, in the direction of a force exerted on it; the greater the force, the more it accelerates, but the more mass the object has, the less it accelerates

**Mass** Amount of matter in an object

**Meteorite** Bit of material that enters Earth from space and falls to the ground

**Microgravity** A nearly weightless condition. The astronauts inside an orbiting spacecraft feel microgravity.

**Newton** Basic unit of force

**Oort Cloud** Huge group of rocks and dust that surround the solar system. This is the home of most comets.

**Orbit** Curving path of an object circling a larger object in space. The Moon follows an orbit around the Earth.

**Orbital velocity** The speed and direction required for a satellite to maintain orbit around Earth and not be pulled in by Earth's gravity

**Particle** Very small piece, or amount, of an object or material

**Revolution** The time it takes for a planet to travel once around the Sun; we call this a year

**Sphere** Object shaped like a ball

**Spring tide** A tide that occurs at the time of a full moon or a new moon. At these times the high tides are higher and the low tides are lower.

**Tides** The alternate rise and fall of the surface of the oceans, seas, bays, and rivers; caused by the attraction of the Sun and the Moon

**Weight** Effect of gravity on mass; weight increases as gravity increases

**X-ray** A form of electromagnetic radiation with great penetrating power

**Zero gravity** A weightless condition in which an object (or person) appears not to be influenced by gravity because other objects in the immediate surroundings are undergoing the same acceleration

# Further Information

## Books to read

Asimov, Isaac. *Black Holes, Pulsars, and Quasars*. Strongsville, OH: Gareth Stevens, 2005.

Farndon, John. *Gravity, Weight, and Balance*. Tarrytown, NY: Marshall Cavendish, 2002.

Olien, Rebecca and Jennifer Way. *Exploring the Planets in Our Solar System*. New York: Rosen Publishing, 2007.

Oxlade, Chris. *Fantastic Forces: Gravity*. Chicago: Heinemann Library, 2007.

Nankivell-Ashton, Sally. *Science Experiments With Forces*. New York: Grolier Publishing, 2000.

Salas, Laura Purdie. *Discovering Nature's Laws: A Story About Isaac Newton*. Minneapolis, MN: Lerner Publishing, 2004

Tocci, Salvatore. *Experiments with Gravity*. Danbury, CT: Children's Press, 2002.

## Websites

http://www.nasa.gov/audience/forstudents/5-8/index.html
*Take a journey with NASA. Travel the galaxy, experience what it's like to be an astronaut, and learn what it takes to be an astrophysicist at this site!*

www.spaceplace.nasa.gov/en/kids/
*Another NASA-sponsored website, with more interesting and fun projects to try.*

http://www.sciencenewsforkids.org
*Find articles, quizzes, games, and more from all types of sciences on this fascinating and informative site!*

## Organizations

**Smithsonian National Air and Space Museum**
National Mall Building
Independence Ave at 6th Street, SW
Washington, DC 20560
http://www.nasm.si.edu/

# Index